TI

G000320318

The Tiny Book of Men Jokes

Fanny Adams

Illustrated by
Frank Dickens

HarperCollins*Publishers*

HarperCollins*Publishers*
77–85 Fulham Palace Road,
Hammersmith, London W6 8JB

www.**fire**and**water**.com

This paperback edition 2001
1 3 5 7 9 8 6 4 2

Previously published in 1996

Copyright © Cathy Hopkins 1996
Illustrations copyright © Frank Dickens 1996

The Author asserts the moral right to
be identified as the author of this work

ISBN 0 00 712875 4

Set in Stone Sans by Rowland Phototypesetting Ltd,
Bury St Edmunds, Suffolk
Printed and bound in Great Britain by Scotprint, Haddington

Three men arrived in heaven and were warned by St Peter that their wings would fall off if they had impure thoughts.

Just then a beautiful blonde went by and the first man's wings fell off.

The second man bent down to pick them up, and the third man's wings fell off.

What's most men's only chance of coming into money?

A girlfriend with gold caps on her teeth.

An Englishman, an Australian and a Scotsman were off to a party.

The Englishman took six bottles of beer, the Australian took six cans of lager, the Scotsman took six of his friends.

Two old blokes were talking about being in the army.

'Hey do you remember that stuff they used to put in our tea to keep our minds off the girls?' asked one.

'Vaguely, it was so long ago,' said the other.

'Well,' said the first, 'I think it's beginning to work.'

Men are like pigeons. They should never be looked up to.

What's a sure sign a man is going to be unfaithful?

He has a penis.

A man was chatting up a woman in a pub and tried his latest chat-up line. 'Hey haven't I seen you somewhere?'

'Yes,' she replied, 'I'm a nurse at the VD clinic.'

In the year 2010, an alien came to earth to buy a brain for research.

The salesman showed him the range.

'First we have the monkey brain,' said the salesman.

'How much?' asked the alien.

'Ten quid,' said the salesman. 'And next we have a woman's brain.'

'How much?' asked the alien.

'A hundred quid,' said the salesman. 'And next we have a man's brain.'

'How much?' asked the alien.

'Five hundred,' said the salesman.

'Why so much?' asked the alien.

'Hardly been used,' said the salesman.

What's the similarity between men and linoleum?

If you lay them right the first time, you can walk on them for life.

A man and his girlfriend were at the movie.

He said: 'Are you comfy?'

She said: 'Yes.'

He said: 'Is there a draught on you?'

She said: 'No.'

He said: 'Can you see OK?'

She said: 'Yes.'

He said: 'Let's change seats.'

A Scotsman was courting a young lassie. One day, they were out in the glen when the young laddie noticed a look of apprehension on the lassie's face. 'Whit's wrang, Jeannie?' he asked. 'Are you afraid o' the gleam in ma e'e?'

'Naw Joch,' she replied, 'it's no the gleam in yer eye – it's the tilt in your kilt.'

What's hard, warm and throbs between a man's legs?

A motorcycle.

LET'S TRY DIFFERENT POSITIONS
O.K....YOU STAND BEHIND THE IRONING BOARD — I'LL LIE O THE COUCH....
SEX MANUAL

What do you call a Welshman with two sheep?
Lucky.
What do you call a Welshman with three sheep?
A pimp.

Two old men were reminiscing about the good old days before promiscuity.

'I certainly never made love to my wife before I was married,' said one. 'Did you?'

'I don't know, old boy,' he replied, 'what was her maiden name?'

How do you get a man to stop biting his nails?
Make him wear his shoes.

Did you hear about the wife who asked her
husband to go and change their young son?
  He was gone for three hours and came back
with a baby girl.

What's the difference between a man and a condom?

Condoms have changed. They're no longer thick and insensitive.

What's long and hard and has semen in it?

A submarine.

What's the definition of hell for men?

A place where there's a lot of beer and girls BUT all the beer mugs have holes and all the girls don't.

What happened to the man who cleared his ears out?

His head caved in.

Did you hear about the man who went to a course for men who suffer from premature ejaculation?

There was no one there.

He was an hour too early.

Who's the most popular man on a nudist beach?

The one who can carry two pina coladas and a dozen pineapple rings all at the same time.

Oh, the grand old Duke of York
He had ten thousand men.
(His court case comes up tomorrow.)

How do you know when a man's had an orgasm?
He's snoring.
How can you tell if a man is sexually excited?
He's breathing.

A man leaned over his girlfriend in their office and said, 'Let's make love.'

'Shhh Michael,' she said, 'you never know who might hear. Let's have a code. Ask instead if you can use my washing machine and I'll know what you mean.'

A few days later, she felt a little romantic and went over to him to whisper, 'Would you like to use my washing machine now?'

'Thanks,' he replied, 'but it was only a small bundle and I've done it by hand.'

What's the similarity between a man and a cheap fireworks display?

One mediocre bang and the evening's over.

A man came into the confessional and said, 'Father I had sex with a pair of stunning eighteen-year-old nymphomaniac twins five times last week.'

'What kind of Catholic are you?' said the priest.

'Oh I'm not Catholic,' the man replied.

'Then why are you telling me this?'

'I'm telling everyone!' the man said.

A small boy went into the bathroom and saw his mother naked.

'What nice balloons you've got, Mum,' he said.

'Why do you call them balloons?' she asked.

''Cos I saw Daddy trying to blow up the nanny's last night.'

What are the three worst things about being a dick?

    1) Your two best mates are nuts and an arsehole

    2) Your master covers you up with a plastic bag

    3) Every time you get excited you throw up

'My sex life is awful,' said the man to his doctor.

The doctor examined him and declared him unfit, and suggested that he jog ten miles a day.

'Give me a ring after a week and let me know how you're getting on,' he said.

A week later his phone rang. 'So how's your sex life now?' asked the doctor.

'How would I know? I'm seventy miles from home,' came the reply.

Two drunken men were walking back across the fields when they spotted a young lamb caught in a fence.

'Ah I wish that was Raquel Welch,' said one. 'What do you wish?'

'I wish it was after dark,' the other replied.

An innocent young man was worried on his wedding night that he didn't know what to do, so he phoned his old mother to ask her.

'Well,' said his mother, 'it's really quite simple. Just put the hardest part of yourself into the place where your wife wee wees.'

Later that night, the hotel manager had to phone the fire brigade. 'Help,' he said. 'We've got a young man here with his head jammed in a toilet bowl.'

Brian and Jack took their wives away for a romantic weekend and had a bet as to who could perform the most.

Jack did it three times and chalked 111 on his door before falling asleep.

Brian staggered down the next morning and said, 'You win mate, one hundred and eleven. Beat me by two.'

Adam came first.

Men always do.

Did you hear about the graffiti left on a condom machine in a men's room?

It read: this gum tastes funny.

Q: What's a man's idea of helping with the housework?

A: Lifting his legs so you can vacuum.

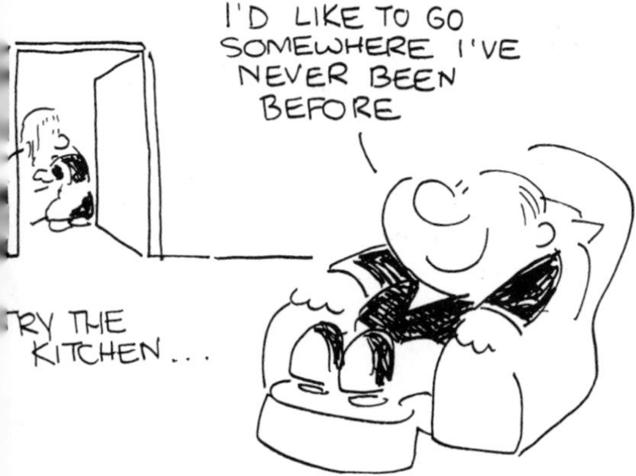
I'D LIKE TO GO SOMEWHERE I'VE NEVER BEEN BEFORE
RY THE KITCHEN . . .

Why do men put women on pedestals?
  So they can look up their skirts.

Why are men who drive taxis the worst lovers?
  Because they never check to see if you're
coming before they pull out.

How do you keep a man from wanting sex all the time?

Marry him.

An unfaithful man staggered home in the early hours of the morning. As he undressed to get into bed, his wife woke up and asked where he'd been.

'And where are your underpants?' she asked, accusingly.

'Oh my God,' he cried, 'I've been robbed.'

Did you hear about the vainest man in the world?
 He shouted his own name when he came.

What happened to the man who put odour
eaters in his shoes?
 He disappeared.

What's the similarity between the average man and a mortgage?

The interest is unwelcome and the demands never end.

Q: What's the difference between a pub and a G spot?

A: A man can always find a pub.

'Mummy, mummy what's an orgasm?'

'How should I know? Shut up and ask your father when he comes home.'

What was the first thing Adam said to Eve?

'Stand back. I don't know how big this thing gets.'

What's the similarity between a man and greasy hair?

Both are lank, limp and lifeless when you want a bit of body.

What's an Englishman's idea of foreplay?
 'Roll over Fiona.'

What's the definition of an ideal husband?
 A guy with a £5 million life insurance policy who dies on your wedding night.

There was a young fellow of Kent
Whose wick was exceedingly bent.
To save himself trouble,
He bent himself double
And instead of coming, he went.

Why did the man put his wife on a pedestal?
So that she could paint the ceiling.

A man went into a chemist and asked for a deodorant.

'The ball type?' asked the assistant.

'No,' he replied, 'it's for my underarms.'

Two old boys met at their club.

'How's your son?' asked the first.

'Great, he's a top salesman,' boasted the father. 'Do you know, the bosses were so pleased with him, they gave him a Mercedes? But he gave it away.'

'My son's the same,' said the first man, 'but he's never lost his generous nature. Top of his profession, his bosses gave him a penthouse to thank him. He gave that away.'

Just then a third man came in and they asked, 'How's your son?'

'Turned out to be a homosexual,' he said gravely, 'still, he's getting on OK, one of his boyfriends gave him a brand new Mercedes. Another gave him a penthouse.'

An Englishman, an American and an Australian were sitting down to a meal with their wives.

'Pass me the sugar, sugar,' said the Englishman to his wife.

Not to be outdone, the American said to his wife, 'Pass me the honey, honey.'

The Australian turned to his wife and said, 'Pass me the tea, bag.'

What's the definition of macho man?

One who jogs home after his own vasectomy.

What do you call a mushroom with a twelve-inch penis?

A fungi to be with.

What's the similarity between men and a game of rugby?

Both play with odd-shaped balls.

A *man's life*
20–30 years tri-weekly
30–50 years try weekly
50–80 years try weakly
over 80 try anything
over 90 try to remember

An old bloke was sitting in the park crying.

'What's up?' asked a passer-by.

'I've got a young wife at home. She's gorgeous, she loves to cook, keeps the place immaculate and is insatiable in bed.'

'So what's the problem?' asked the passer-by.

'I can't remember where I live,' sobbed the old guy.

A man went to a doctor.

'My hair is falling out. Can you give me anything for it?' he asked.

The doctor gave him a box.

Why do Irishmen wear two condoms during sex?

To be sure, to be sure.

Two businessmen were having a drink.

'There're lots of ways of making money,' said one, 'but only one honest way.'

'What's that?' said the other.

'Hah!' said the first. 'I knew you wouldn't know.'

There priests went to buy a train ticket. The girl behind the counter had enormous breasts with a deep cleavage.

'Three tickets to Titterton,' stuttered the first, then retired with embarrassment.

'Three titties to Tockerton,' said the second, getting even more embarrassed.

'Let me do it,' said the third in disgust. 'Three tickets to Tottenham, Miss. And unless you dress more demurely St Finger will point his Peter at you.'

Milady rang for the butler. When he arrived, she said:

'Soames take off my coat.

Soames take off my dress.

Soames take off my stockings.

Soames take off my bra.

And Soames, never let me catch you wearing them again!'

D id you hear about the man who stayed in bed
for fourteen days and nights on his honeymoon?
Afterwards his new wife was exhausted.

He, however, got up feeling very pleased with
himself and boasted, 'I feel like a new man.'

'So do I,' said his bride.

 W hat are the three lies that men tell?

I'll call you.

I love you.

I promise I won't come in your mouth.

A newly married man was looking forward to his wedding night.

'Now we're married at last darling,' said his wife, 'will you tell me what a penis is?'

The man led her into the bedroom and he proudly took down his trousers to show her.

'Oh!' she exclaimed, 'like a prick only smaller.'

DAD — ARE YOU STILL GROWING?
NO — WHY DO YOU ASK?
THE TOP OF YOUR HEAD IS COMING THROUGH YOUR HAIR. . .

What's the correct term for when an Englishman's girlfriend has an orgasm?

A miracle.

An American asked a Scotsman if there was anything worn under his kilt.

'Nope. All complete and in working order,' said the Scot proudly.

Two girls were in a cinema:

'Oh no,' said one, 'the man next to me is masturbating.'

'Just ignore him,' said her friend.

'I can't,' she replied, 'he's using my hand.'

Did you hear about the two gay Irishmen?

Patrick Fitzwilliam and William Fitzpatrick.

Did you hear about the two Scottish homosexuals?

Ben Doon and Phil MacAvity.

A man came back to bed and proclaimed he'd just seen a miracle.

'When I went to the bathroom the light came on all by itself, then when I'd finished, the light went off all by itself,' he said.

'No miracle,' replied his girlfriend, 'you're drunk and you've peed in the refrigerator again.'

A man at a nudist colony got a letter from his mother asking him to send a photo. As the only picture he had was of him in the nude, he cut it in half and sent the top half showing him from the waist up.

After a week, his mother wrote back asking if he would send another picture for his grandma.

The man thought that since his grandmother couldn't see too well, he could send her the bottom half of the picture and she'd never be any the wiser. He sent it off the next day.

A week later, he received a letter from his grandma. 'Nice picture,' it read, 'but your new hairstyle makes your nose look long.'

What's the definition of a faithful husband?
 One whose alimony cheques arrive on time.

What's the similarity between a man and a video recorder?
 Play, fast forward, pause and eject.

W hat's an Australian man's idea of foreplay?
'You awake?'

W hat's an Australian man's idea of seduction?
'Brace yourself. I'm coming in.'

A genie appeared to a man and said he would grant him one wish.

'I want a penis that touches the floor,' said the man.

Kersham! And his legs fell off.

Jack be nimble, Jack be quick
Jack jump over the candlestick
Alas, he didn't clear the flame
And now he's known as Aunty Maime.

What do you call a man who uses the withdrawal method of contraception?

Daddy.

What's the similarity between an Englishman and a football player?

They both dribble when they're trying to score.

What's the definition of an average man?
One who thinks he isn't.

FIRST MAN: 'My mother made me a homosexual.'
SECOND MAN: 'If I get the wool, would she make me one too?'

What's the only thing the government can't tax? A penis, because ninety per cent of the time it's inactive, ten per cent of the time it's in a hole, and it's got two dependants and they're both nuts.

Did you hear about the woman who gave birth to a freak baby? It had the organs of both sexes. A penis *and* a brain.

'Does your husband lie awake at night?'
   'Yes, and he lies in sleep too.'

What's the similarity between an Englishman and a bus?
   Neither comes when you want them then just as you're about to give up, they come all at once.

Why is a Catholic man like a British Rail train?
  Neither pull out on time.

What's the difference between a Scotsman and
a coconut?
  You can get a drink out of a coconut.

The French were to guillotine three men. Each prisoner could choose whether to lie under it face up, or face down.

The first man chose face up.

The blade got caught just short of his throat and he was allowed to go free.

The second man also chose face up and the same thing happened to him. He too was allowed to go free.

The third man also chose face up.

He lay ready when suddenly he said: 'Hold on a minute. I think I see what your trouble is.'

A man told his doctor he could only achieve climax in doggie position.

'So what's the problem?' asked the doctor.

'The dog's got bad breath,' replied the man.

A young lad was out watching his dad play golf.

'Why is it that the ball must never go in the hole Dad?' he asked.

A wife asked her husband for some shopping money.

'Money!' he shouted, 'money? You're always asking for money. If you ask me, I think you need brains more than money.'

'Yes dear,' she agreed, 'but I thought I'd ask you for what you had most of.'

What's the similarity between a man and a packet of condoms?

They both come in three sizes. Small, medium and liar.

What's the definition of a cad?

A man who doesn't tell his wife he's sterile until after she's pregnant.

What's the similarity between a man and a bad cello player?

They both sit and scratch their instrument instead of learning to use it properly.

Fred has a musical nature
He can yodel, whistle and hum
He goes out fit as a fiddle,
And he comes home tight as a drum.

SON: 'Dad, does God use our bathroom?'

DAD: 'Why do you ask that?'

SON: 'Cos this morning, I heard you shout, "God are you still in there?"'

PADDY: 'Hey Mick, if you can guess how many chickens I have in this bag, you can have both of them.'

MICK: 'Er . . . Three?'

Four men in hell were queuing up to see the devil.

'First,' yelled the devil.

'I don't know why I'm here,' said the first. 'I've led a good life.'

'Over in the shed,' said the devil. 'Take your clothes off and wait.'

'Next,' shouted the devil.

The next two men are the same – good men, honest and true.

'In the shed, take off your clothes and wait,' said the devil.

The fourth man confessed that he was a drunk, a thief, a gambler, a cheat.

'Right,' said the devil. He pointed at the shed. 'I'll just burn that lot then we'll go for a pint.'

A man went to the doctor.

'Can you give me anything for my wind?' he asked.

The doctor gave him a kite.

What do you call a man who marries another man?

A priest.

A man arrived at the Pearly Gates.

'What good works have you done?' asked St Peter.

The man thought for a moment. 'Well,' he said, 'the other day, I gave a beggar in town twenty pence.'

'Anything else?'

'Once when I was young, I gave a poor man ten pence.'

'Gabriel,' shouted Peter, 'is it in the record?'

'Yep, all here,' said Gabriel.

'What shall I do with him?'

'Give him back his thirty pence, said Gabriel.

'What!' said Peter.

'. . . and tell him to go to hell.'

What's the similarity between men and old age?
  They both come too soon.

What's the similarity between sex with a man
and a bank account?
  After withdrawal, they both lose interest.

A sailor was confused when his wife became pregnant so he went to the doctor.

'She can't be pregnant,' he said. 'I haven't seen her for two years.'

'It's what we call a grudge pregnancy,' explained the doctor.

'What's that?' the sailor asked.

'It's when someone has it in for you.'

Father and son were posing for a photo at the son's graduation.

'Stand close,' said the photographer to the father, 'and put your hand on his shoulder.'

'Wouldn't it be more appropriate if he put his hand in my pocket?' said the father.

What's the similarity between a man and the local council?

Impossible to get through to either when you need to talk.

Why can't men think straight?

Because they've always got curves on their mind.

What's the soft fleshy material that surrounds a penis called?

A man.

A man was in bed with his lover when suddenly she cried out that husband was home.

'Quick – in the bathroom,' she cried.

Without time to collect his clothes, he hid behind a shower curtain.

The husband burst into the bedroom and then the bathroom. Pulling back the curtain he found the man naked, clapping and snatching at the air.

'What are you doing?' demanded the husband.

'I'm a moth catcher,' the lover said breathlessly, 'your wife called me in.'

'But why aren't you wearing any clothes?'

'Blimey,' said the man, 'the buggers are worse than I thought.'

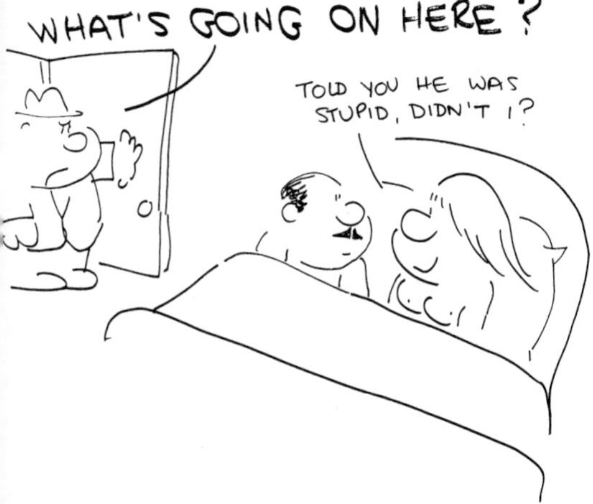
WHAT'S GOING ON HERE?
TOLD YOU HE WAS STUPID, DIDN'T I?

Plumber: 'Where's the drip?'
    Wife: 'In the bathroom trying to fix the leak.'

What's the similarity between a man and a riding stable?
    Both are either vacant or full of shit.

What do men think oral contraception is?
Talking your way out of it.

Why is an erection like the theory of relativity?
The more you think about it, the harder it gets.

A Scotsman decided to try it on with his new shy girlfriend and lifted his kilt.

'Ugh,' she said, 'that's gruesome.'

'Aye,' he said proudly, 'and now I'll show you how it can gruesome more.'

Did you hear about the man who told his wife that black underwear turned him on?

So she didn't wash his pants for three months.

There were two signs outside heaven.

A long line of men queued in front of the first one, a sign which read: 'Henpecked husbands report here.'

At the other sign which read, 'Liberated men stand here,' there was only one man.

St Peter said to him: 'Why are you standing here?'

'My wife told me to,' he replied meekly.

What does a man do on his fiancée's hen night?
Gets his pecker out.

A knight was setting out on a crusade. Before he left he locked his wife into a chastity belt and left the key in his trusted best friend's keeping.

'If I'm not back in two years, let her out,' he said.

He then started off on his journey.

Twenty minutes later his friend had caught up with him.

'What's wrong?' he asked.

'You gave me the wrong key,' his friend panted.

A pansy by name of Ben Bloom
Took a lesbian up to his room
They talked the whole night
As to who had the right
To do what, with which, and to whom.

A man had been stung on the penis by a bee. His wife sent him to the doctor with a note on which she had written:

'Dear Doctor, please take out the sting but leave the swelling in.'

A woman took the ashes of her recently cremated husband to the top of a sky scraper, where she threw them out into an oncoming gust of wind.

'There's that blow job I always promised you,' she said.

MAN: (after argument) 'I'll meet you halfway.'

WOMAN: 'How?'

MAN: 'I'll admit I'm wrong if you admit that I'm right.'

How does a pervert expose himself to culture? He flashes in the local art gallery.

Why do most men need two women?

A secretary to take things down and a wife to pick things up.

What is it called if you marry two men?

Bigamy.

What is it called if you marry one man?

Monotony.

There's only one thing that stops him being a bare-faced liar.

What's that?

His moustache.

How many Australian chauvinists does it take to change a light bulb?

None. Let the bitch cook in the dark.

A man wrote in his diary, 'I am the perfect man. I don't smoke or drink or gamble or stay out late. I am completely faithful to my wife. I go to bed early and rise early. I work regular hours and exercise daily.

Of course all this will change when I get out of jail.'

What's an Australian man's idea of the perfect woman?

3ft high, large mouth and a flat head to rest your beer on.

There once was a man from Blatz
Whose balls were constructed of glass.
When they clanked together
They played Stormy Weather
And lightning shot out of his ass.

What excuse do some men give for never taking their wives out?

It's wrong to go out with married women.

Dick was out with his mistress one night and he fell asleep . . .

He was reluctant to call home as he knew his wife would guess what he'd been up to, and he had an idea.

He rang his wife; 'Don't pay the ransom,' he shouted down the phone. 'I escaped.'

How can you tell if a man is lying?
His lips move.

Did you hear about the man who said he wouldn't stand for sexual harassment in his office?

He asked his secretary to lie on the desk.

'Why don't you let me know when you have an orgasm?' a man asked his girlfriend.

'I would, but you're never there,' she replied.

When a husband came home unexpectedly, his wife's lover had to leap naked through the window. Spotting some joggers, he quickly joined them.

'Do you always jog in the nude?' asked one.

'Oh yes,' he replied, 'it's very stimulating.'

'And do you usually jog with a condom on?' asked another.

'Not always,' the lover replied, 'but it was raining when I set out.'

Did you hear about the man who brought home a tube of KY jelly for his girl, saying it would make her happy.

It did.

She put some on the doorknob when he went to the bathroom, and he couldn't get back in.

Graffiti in men's loo:

It's no good looking for a joke.

You've got one in your hand.

Why don't smart men make good husbands?
Because smart men never get married.

A man was asked to take a paternity test.
  'And were you the father?' asked a friend later.
  'They'll never find out,' he replied, 'they took
samples from my finger.'

A man took his girl to the cinema on their third date, and he decided to get a bit frisky. He leant over, took his girlfriend's hand, put it on his willie and whispered in her ear, 'This is for you.'

'Not now thanks,' she said, 'but I'll put it behind my ear and smoke it later.'

What's the similarity between a man and a balloon?

Both are full of hot air.

What do men think about vasectomies?
   That a stitch in time saves nine.

A mathematician named Paul
Has a hexahedronical ball
And the cube of its weight
Times his pecker plus eight
Is his phone number –
Give him a call.

A young athlete was doing push ups when a drunk staggered past then came back and laughed at him.

'What's so funny?' said the athlete puffing away.

'Hate to tell you,' sniggered the drunk, 'but your girlfriend's gone home.'

A sociologist was collecting data about how often people make love.

'How many make love more than once a week?' he asked a crowd.

Five raised their hands.

'Twice a month?'

Ten raised their hands.

'Once a year?'

A man at the back happily waved his hand.

'If only once a year, why so happy?'

'Tonight's the night,' he replied excitedly.

There was a young fellow named Bill
Who took a mind-blowing pill
His entrails corroded
His belly exploded
And his balls were found in Brazil.

There was an old fellow from Cosham
Who took out his bollocks to wash 'em.
His wife said: 'Now Jack
If you don't put 'em back
I shall jump on the beggars and squash 'em.'

What's a man's idea of safe sex?
Masturbation.

The young actor rushed home to tell his dad he'd got a job.

'I play a man who's been married thirty years,' he said excitedly.

'Never mind son, eventually you'll get a speaking part,' said his dad.

What's the average man's mating call?
  I'll pay for dinner.

What's the definition of a bachelor?
  A man who comes to work every morning from a different direction.

What's long and pink
  And red in parts
  And sometimes used
  to put in tarts?
  Rhubarb.

What's the most insensitive part of the penis?
  The man.

What's the difference between a snowman and a snowwoman?
  Snowballs.

In the Garden of Eden lay Adam
Graciously stroking his madam
And loud was his mirth
For on all of the earth
There were only two balls
And he 'ad 'em.

There once was a fellow from Pinner
Whose penis began to grow thinner,
After several days
It was useless for lays
But for pipe cleaning it was a winner.

'Young man, you are accused of stealing a petticoat.'

    'It was my first slip officer.'

A man went into a shop to see if they had a cure for his persistent erection.

'Help,' he said to the young female assistant, 'I've had this erection for three weeks now and it still hasn't gone down. What can you give me for it?'

She disappeared, saying she had to go and ask someone out the back.

Moments later, she returned.

'I've talked it over with my mate and the best we can do is a cheque for two hundred and fifty pounds.'

Fred was reading about the world's population.

'Did you know every time I breathe in and out someone dies?' he asked.

'Ever tried mouthwash?' replied his friend.

What's a puff adder?

A man who farts in the bath then counts the bubbles.

A parish priest went to a house swarming with kids. He knocked on the door but he got no answer, so he looked through a window and was shocked to see two people making love on the bed.

Embarrassed, he made a hasty retreat and went next door.

'Your neighbours sure like making babies,' he commented to the man of the house.

'Yes,' said the man, 'in fact, his wife is in hospital having her tenth. My wife is over at the house now helping him out.'

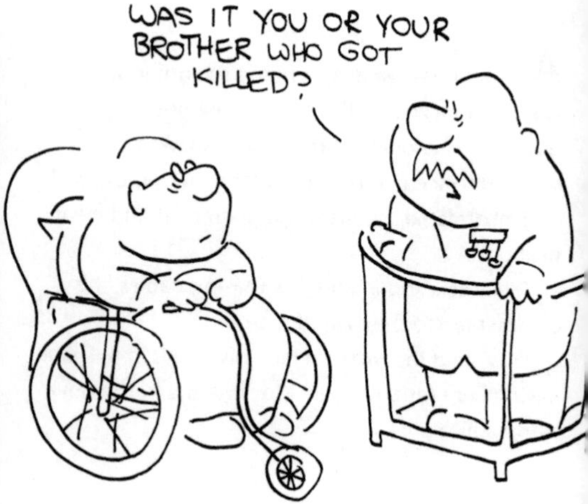
WAS IT YOU OR YOUR BROTHER WHO GOT KILLED?

What do you call a Chinese man with a venereal disease?

Ping pong balls.

Did you hear about the man who left his body to science?

Science is contesting the will.

Two men were coming home late at night and had missed their last train so they decided to steal a bus.

One of them hopped onto the 39.

'Come on, get on,' he called to his friend.

'No use to me mate,' the other called back, 'I'd be OK to the junction then I'd have to change to a 103.'

What's the similarity between a man and a *Reader's Digest* mail shot?

Both promise to make dreams come true but only deliver more demands.

What do most men think about circumcision?
That it's a rip-off.

Why do unfaithful men rarely get haemorrhoids?
Because they are perfect arseholes.

A man went into a pub and said, 'Quick, give me
a beer before the fight starts.'

The barman pulled a pint and the man gulped it
down.

'Another, quick, before the fight starts.'

Again the barman pulled him a pint and the
man downed it fast.

'So when's this fight going to start?' asked the
barman.

'Any moment now,' said the man. 'I've got no
money.'

What did the man say to the girl who told him that her body was her temple?

That he'd like to attend more services.

WAITRESS: 'Say when.'

MAN: 'Right after this drink.'

Why is kissing a man like a spider's web?

It results in the undoing of flies.

What is it six men can do at once that three women can't?

Pee simultaneously into the same bucket.

When's the only time you can change a man?

When he's a baby.

FIRST MAN: Would you like a ticket for the local policeman's ball?

SECOND MAN: No thanks, I can't dance.

FIRST MAN: It's not a dance, it's a raffle.

What goes in dry, comes out wet and gives a lot of pleasure?

A tea bag.

There men were captured by a barbaric tribe in a jungle.

The first man's torture was have raisins put up his backside.

The second man broke out into a grin when he saw what his torturer had lined up for him. A big bowl of oranges.

'Why are you smiling? Aren't you frightened?' asked the first man in amazement.

'Not now I've seen what our third man's in for,' he replied.

Last in the line of torturers was a man waiting for the third prisoner with a large bowl of cactus fruit.

What do you call a man in a bog?
  Pete.

First God made Adam.
  Then God made Eve.
  Then He stood back and said 'Practice makes perfect.'

CHILD: Mummy, why do all fairy stories start with 'Once upon a time'?

MOTHER: Not all of them do, darling. Some start with 'Bloody traffic held me up again . . .'

Jesus was a typical man – they all say they'll be back and that's the last you see of them.

What do you call a man with no arms in the swimming pool?

Bob.

What do you call a man with a seagull on his head?

Cliff.

'I'll never forget Father's Day last year.

'I called my dad to wish him a happy Father's Day, and we had a conversation that made me feel closer than ever to him. We talked about when he was young, when he first met my mother, Christmas, birthdays, how he really felt about things, and then before I hung up, he said three little words which I'll never forget.

'He said, "Who are you?" '

What goes in hard and dry and comes out wet and soft?

Chewing gum.

What four-letter words do men find most offensive?

'Don't' and 'Stop'.

Why does the Pope wear his underpants in the bath?

Because it upsets him to see the unemployed.

A man was in a very posh hotel when he let out a loud fart. Embarrassed, he decided to blame it on the waiter.

'Waiter, stop that,' he said.

'Certainly sir,' said the waiter, 'which way did it go.'

Three people were in a lift. The perfect man, the perfect woman and Father Christmas. There was a five pound note on the floor. Who bent down to pick it up?

The perfect woman of course. Everyone knows the other two don't exist.